PLACE, ART, AND SELF

PLACE, ART, AND SELF

YI-FU TUAN

WITH PHOTOGRAPHS BY TAMMY MERCURE,
JOCELYN NEVEL, JOHN WILLIS, AND TOM YOUNG

Santa Fe, New Mexico, and Staunton, Virginia

in association with

Columbia
COLLEGE CHICAGO

PUBLISHER'S NOTES:

Place, Art, and Self is brought to publication in an edition of 1,750 softcover copies, with the generous financial assistance of the Friends of the Center for American Places and Columbia College Chicago, for which the publisher is most grateful. The Center commissioned the book, which Professor Tuan first presented publicly as a lecture at Princeton University on 8 October 2003.

Design by Colleen Dahlberg Plumb
plumbimage@earthlink.net

Center for American Places, Inc.
P.O. Box 23225
Santa Fe, New Mexico 87502, U.S.A.
www.americanplaces.org

Distributed by the University of Virginia Press
www.upress.virginia.edu

9 8 7 6 5 4 3 2 1
Library of Congress Cataloging-in-Publication Data is available from the publisher upon request.

ISBN 1-930066-24-4

Cover: John Willis and Tom Young
Frontispiece: Tammy Mercure
Back Cover: Kevin Cassidy, with the permission of
           Philip Greenspun http://philipgreenspun.com

"MY FATHER WAS VERY SURE ABOUT CERTAIN THINGS PERTAINING TO THE UNIVERSE. TO HIM, ALL GOOD THINGS—TROUT AS WELL AS ETERNAL SALVATION—COME BY GRACE AND GRACE COMES BY ART AND ART DOES NOT COME EASY."

–NORMAN MACLEAN, from
A River Runs through It

CONTENTS

ACKNOWLEDGMENTS

I would like to acknowledge my three principal sources of inspiration for this chapbook: my colleague at the University of Wisconsin-Madison, Robert David Sack, a philosophical geographer of exceptional originality; the Committee on Public Lectures at Princeton University, which honored me with an invitation to deliver the J. Edward Farnum Lecture on 8 October 2003; and George F. Thompson and Randall B. Jones, respectively, president and associate editorial director of the Center for American Places. George and Randy are co-begetters of this book in that they contributed ideas to it and edited it. George and Bob Thall, chairman of the Photography Department at Columbia College Chicago, then selected and sequenced the illustrations for it. Whatever merit the book has owes much to them. As for its deficiencies, especially those in the main text, I, as its author, am solely responsible.

I have another reason to express my gratitude to George Thompson, which is that he has for some time encouraged me to tackle a large topic in a small book. This suits me perfectly, for I am constrained by both temperament and energy level to be a short-distance runner in any enterprise, including the scholarly. The exhaustive treatise, much as I admire it, is not for me. Truth to tell, even reading one can make me feel stuffed, brow-beaten, and a little depressed rather than exhilarated and energized. I much prefer the little book—the exploratory essay that gives the reader room to argue and develop ideas of his or her own. My fond wish is that *Place, Art, and Self* is such a book.

PLACE, ART, AND SELF

PROLOGUE

Geographers are concerned with place, artists and art historians with art, psychologists and philosophers with self. What do place, art, and self have in common? To what extent do place and art define who we are? I propose to explore these topics, beginning with the human attachment to place. How firm is it and how does it vary from person to person? Place — geographical place — is a material environment. It can be natural, as, for example, an unspoiled forest or seashore; and it can be — to varying degree — artifactual, everything from a thatched hut to a glass-and-steel high rise. In the process of considering place as an architectural artwork, we may be led to ask whether other artworks such as a painting, photograph, poem, story, movie, dance, or musical composition can also be a place — a virtual place. Isn't it true that we pause before them, rest in them, and are, in one sense of another, nurtured by them, as we rest and are nurtured by the towns and cities and landscapes we live in or visit?

The word "nurture" says two things about us: that we "feed" on places and artworks, and that, so fed, we grow. The self, in other words, is not fixed. We continue to discover who we are as we open ourselves to new sources of nurture and experience. Obvious as this sounds, it needs restatement in order to counter the fashionable view, which finds surprising acceptance even in mobile America, that somehow a firm sense of self depends on being rooted. Of course, a degree of stability must hold for place and art to work their magic. But rootedness is not the answer if only because it sets the self into a mold too soon. Mobility carried to excess, on the other hand, makes it difficult, if not impossible, for a strong sense of self to jell. A self that is coherent and firm, yet capable of growth, would seem to call for an alternation of stillness and motion, stability and change, place and space, the duration of each being calibrated by culture and individual temperament. One more point has to be made, which is that being rooted in place and feeling wholly at ease there is unambiguously good only from an earthbound religious, or secular, point of view. In faiths driven by insatiable yearning, such at-homeness signifies a deadening of the spirit.

LAMB, LARKIN, AND WILLIAMS

Let me return to my initial question, which is, "How firmly or lightly are people attached to place?" Representing the firm end are the testimonies of Charles Lamb (1775-1834) and Philip Larkin (1922-1985); representing the light end is the testimony of Hugo Williams (b. 1942). Lamb wrote: "I am in love with this green earth; the face of town and country; the unspeakable rural solitudes, and the sweet security of streets. I would set up my tabernacle here. I am content to stand still at the age to which I am arrived; I and my friends: to be no younger, no richer, no handsomer. I do not want to be weaned by age...Any alteration, on this earth of mine, in diet or lodging, puzzles and decomposes me. My household gods plant a terrible fixed foot, and are not rooted up without blood."[1] More matter-of-factly, Larkin opined: "I wouldn't mind seeing China if I could come back the same day. I hate being abroad. Generally speaking, the further one gets from home the greater the misery."[2]

At the opposite pole from Lamb and Larkin is the much younger man, Hugo Williams. "I hate landscaping my life as far as the eye can see," he said when he was twenty-one. Rather than make plans for a post-college world tour, he left chance to decide pretty much where he was to be next. At Haifa, he stopped at shipping offices in the hope of finding work. "I didn't care in which direction I went," he recalled, "as any voyage would have taken me on my way." At one point in his aimless drifting, he found himself at the mouth of the Tigris and the Euphrates rivers. It was late in the night. The boat put down anchor. Passengers relaxed. Williams noted:

[A] little man in striped pantaloons soon produced from his pocket a little pellet of hashish, wrapped up in silver paper. He made a cigarette and offered me a smoke. I pretended to know how to do it and sucked the tobacco through my clenched fist. This made me very popular and the cigarette kept being passed back to me till I could feel the drug in my scalp, seething about under my hair. Then it settled down and I was able to enjoy the warm night, the fireflies like lovely fat stupid virgins giving themselves away to the night birds, the bobbing, luminous floats of the fisher boats, the shooting stars between the masts, the laughs in a strange language. For the first time I noticed how very far I was getting from home and experienced almost physical pleasure at the thought.[3]

THE TUG OF PLACE AND SPACE

Reading these and other accounts have made me wonder, "Where do I put myself on the scale of attachment to place?" My own life path shows that I am neither rooted like Lamb and Larkin, nor driven to tramp the world like Williams. Yet I not only understand, but can feel the tug of both positions. It may be that, whatever people say and even do, such bipolar tug is common. It is, in fact, human. Lamb and Larkin must have known — sometime — the call of open space, just as Williams must have known the call of home. On the attachment scale, points in the middle range are necessarily ambiguous, but I have come to see that the extremities are not as firm as I thought, for they contain the seed of their opposite. Take home. To the young child, it is not only a familiar and nurturing place, it is also a space that invites exploration. Grown-ups forget that, when they were little, a trip to the attic or basement could be an adventure and that camping overnight in the backyard had the same sort of thrill they now have camping in the wilds of the Adirondacks or Alaska. The special appeal of our childhood home, as distinct from homes we have occupied later in life, lies in its catering to the bipolar pull of our nature.

As for the restless spirits, perhaps even more than other people they need the succor of home, if only as the point of departure. Some of the world's greatest explorers have left accounts of home whose mawkishness contrasts sharply with the cool prose they use to describe hair-raising adventures and excruciating hardships. Here is the Norwegian explorer, Fridtjof Nansen, noting how he felt as he left home for the motor launch that would take him to the ship *Fram*, which in turn was to take him and his crew to the North Pole. "Behind me lay all I held dear in life. And what before me? How many years would pass ere I should see it all again? What would I not have given at that moment to be able to turn back..."[4] Hibernating with F. H. Johansen in their hut on Franz Josef Land, Nansen thought of his wife and daughter. He wrote in his diary (19 December 1895): "There she sits in the winter's evening, sewing by lamplight. Beside her stands a young girl with blue eyes and golden hair playing with a doll. She looks tenderly at the child... Her eyes grow moist, and heavy tears fall on to her sewing... Here beside me lies Johansen asleep. He is smiling in his sleep. Poor boy, I expect he is at home spending Christmas with those he loves."[5]

An explorer's camp is home, primitive no doubt, but all the

more homelike by contrast with nature's indifference and hostility. Leaving camp on 29 October 1908, for the track to the South Pole, Ernest Shackleton wrote: "As we left the hut where we had spent so many months in comfort, we had a feeling of real regret... It was dark inside, the acetylene was feeble in comparison with the sun outside, and it was small compared to an ordinary dwelling, yet we were sad leaving it. Last night as we were sitting at dinner the evening sun entered through the ventilator and a circle of light shone on the picture of the Queen..."[6]

JOURNEY AND ITS PAUSES

If we feel a certain fascination for explorers and exploration, it may be because all of us are embarked on the journey of life. We are on the move, one that is relieved by pauses, each of which produces a somewhat familiar world — a place, even if this is just a camp in the Arctic wilds; the longer pauses produce homes or home-like places. While this is a good enough characterization of our journey through space, it fits less well with our journey through time. In the journey through time, there is no pause, not even in sleep. We become older every second and move inexorably to our final destination — death. Recognizing this fact makes us anxious, and so we don't, unless we are philosophically inclined. For most of us, time, rather than moving forward smoothly and steadily, is punctuated by stases during which we seem hardly to move or age at all: young children, for example, feel that a year is an eternity, and though young adulthood passes quickly, once middle-age is reached, time dawdles so that, even as the years roll implacably by, we see little change in ourselves. At the level of common experience, then, both space and time can seem discontinuous.

Stases are needed to recuperate, but also to take stock of what the world is like and who we are. What is the world like? It is mostly made up of stable, material things — mallets that stay put, Alice might say, so that she can play croquet properly. As for our identity, it is anchored in common objects and experiences to a degree we seldom acknowledge. Think how posture is shaped by furniture, spatial intuition tutored by the daily triangulation of tree, telephone pole, and fence in the backyard, sensorial memories added to, on a regular basis, by the skyline silhouetted against the evening sky, bedroom ceilings in tenement houses glowing darkly under street neon signs, the faint aroma of clothes drying in the sun and the pungent odor of gas fumes exuding from a passing school bus, the sound of lawnmowers in summer and of snow blowers in winter.

CHANGE AND IDENTITY

Home is a house and, in the larger sense, a neighborhood, hometown, country — and, ultimately, the earth. Our identity expands and is enriched as the places in which we feel at home — if only temporarily — are multiplied. This seems to say that identity changes over time, that we are one sort of person when young and another sort when mature or old. Though obviously true as judged by certain objective measures, subjectively we may feel that, through it all, we remain essentially the same person. Are we or are we not the same person? Do we lose our integrity if we change? That a child's self is unformed and fluid doesn't bother us, for childhood is properly the time to try on different roles. But maturity, if it means anything, means that we know at last who we are. We cannot have integrity, act dependably so that others can depend on us, unless we have a stable self.

Change is clearly good if it means putting away childish things. But change as loss and disintegration in life's downward path to death is unwelcome. This ambiguity toward change in the self is carried over toward change in the environment, which is understandable, given the intimate bond between the two. In a confused and contradictory way, we want the world we live in and ourselves to show both integrity and dynamism, our neighborhood to retain the character of fond memories, yet our town or city to prosper and grow.

The degree that we can have both depends in part on scale. A place of the size of a city can change radically within a decade. Take downtown Minneapolis, my home for fourteen years. I left it for Madison, Wisconsin, in 1983. In the next three to four years, I could still regard Minneapolis as home. And then it became impossible. Too many new skyscrapers sprouted up in the 1980s, displacing or totally dwarfing the landmarks I knew. In their absence, the years I lived there have lost shape, detail, and vividness. As the city is no longer quite the same city, so I — with the blurring of an important period of my past — am no longer quite the same person. Yet if I consider not Minneapolis but the State of Minnesota as home, it (the State) still supports my sense of self, for though its cities have grown and more highways now thread it, the 10,000 lakes that give Minnesota its physical character remain more or less intact. Beyond country and nation-state are still larger entities that may be considered home, culminating in the earth, home for all living things. Increasingly, people believe that the integrity of the earth itself is under threat—a belief that is fueled by disturbing images and reports from outer space. For example, Astronaut Frank Culbertson told us in September of 2001 that, from his window in the international space station, he could see that our planet has more dust and smoke, and less forested areas, since his last mission in 1990.[7] Even after a short lapse of time, Culbertson must have felt that he cannot return home—to a cleaner earth—again. In some people's minds, the question arises whether such deterioration of the global ecosystem can continue without affecting the physical and moral soundness of the human species as a whole.

A STATE OF BEING

I have been emphasizing the importance of place—the ties to place. But if so, why do so many people look forward to traveling? Is the movement—is being in transit—itself enjoyable, or does true satisfaction lie in the pauses, encounters, and states of being that can occur, sometimes unexpectedly, in the course of travel? Pilgrimage is, of course, directed to a goal, the journey being merely the means to it. But is travel for pleasure all that different? It, too, has to terminate in a desirable place. True, the word "tour," as in the Caribbean tour, suggests otherwise. Yet one may still wonder: Are not the exotic ports of call the high points in any tour? If they are not, if being on the ship as it moves through the waters is the more rewarding experience, isn't this because the ship itself has become a place, able to offer comfort and stimulation?

The importance of a place depends notably on how long we have lived or worked in it. Permanent places accumulate more sentiment and play a greater role in our sense of self than do places we merely visit, or pass through. Yet there are exceptions. A major motivation for travel—hardships notwithstanding—is the vague expectation of entering a state of being, identified with a particular place or landscape, that, however transient, reveals an aspect of our character that we have not previously known.

Consider, again, Hugo Williams. He bummed around the world, staying in small villages and big cities as chance and opportunity took him. No doubt these places had significance—some anticipated—for him: after all, one can hardly go to Mecca or Alice Springs without anticipating certain kinds of experience. Still, among the most memorable were unplanned God-sends. His night at the mouth of the Tigris and Euphrates was one. What a moment of self-revelation it must have been for this young man to realize that home could be a small boat in the Middle East, inhaling hashish, awash in the sound of his fellow passengers speaking a language he doesn't understand, looking up at a night sky filled with stars, and about him at the smooth water dotted with lights from other boats.

Williams hated "landscaping his life" to as far as the eyes can see. I, for my part, have always wanted to landscape my life for fear of disorientation and worse. At Williams's age, I seldom did anything without purpose. I traveled as widely as he, but always with a goal in mind. Yet the unexpected did happen. Most of them I could do without. A few I embraced as gifts out of the blue, revealing aspects of me to myself that would otherwise remain hidden. These gifts usually came to me in human shape or as artwork. Once, however, it came as a landscape. During winter break, 1952, some Chinese students and I decided that we should try that all-American pastime—camping out. We left Berkeley for Death Valley National Monument early one morning in the expectation that we would get there before dark. Our car broke down in Fresno and took hours to fix. It was late in the night when we arrived at our destination. A strong wind rose that made our amateurish attempts at raising a tent futile. In the end, we simply slept in our sleeping bags, exposed to the wind and the dust. I slept soundly. Opening my eyes many hours later, I was shocked into full wakefulness by lunar beauty. The first rays of the morning sun turned the Valley's west wall into a phantasmagoria of shimmering mauves, purples, and golds. Extraterrestrial, too, were the saline flats on the Valley floor, immaculately white, and stark sculptural reliefs unsoiled by life.

PLACE AND THE ARTS

Death Valley is a tourist attraction. Many go there for its visual novelty—its strangeness. For me, it has always been far more. In my very first encounter with the desert, I felt as though I had met my geographical double—the objective correlative of the person I am, absent the social facade. I didn't make much of the experience at the time, but as the years passed, I began to wonder how it compared with my encounters with works of art. More generally, I wondered about the kinship between place and the arts—not so much how certain places seem to encourage art, or how the arts have influenced the way we perceive place, but how the arts themselves are places—virtual places.

Hints of their kinship are many. Figures of speech that might be applied to place such as "a quiet pool in the river of time" or "a rest stop in the journey of life" apply equally well to certain genres of art. Place is a center of meaning—primarily positive meaning. The same can be said of art.[8] Place is different things to different people, as, of course, is art. Some people take place and art seriously; they may make a conscious effort to preserve or enrich them. Others are indifferent, but this is more apparent than real: witness the feeling of laceration when, for some reason, they have to leave a familiar place; witness, also, their attachment to comely objects—comely as they see it—and their readiness to use the expletive 'shit!' when their world threatens to become too chaotic, threatening, or unaesthetic.

Consciously or subconsciously, place is felt to have import. The ultimate sources of this feeling are nurture and identity. At a minimum, place offers shade and water, one example being the water hole in the desert, another being a rest stop by the highway. As for the arts, why do we dwell on them if they don't, in some sense, feed and strengthen us? A painter's special challenge, Bernard Berenson once noted, is "to convey, more rapidly and unfailingly than nature would do, the consciousness of an unusually intense degree of well-being."[9] I read him to say that, if a fine wine can make us feel good, a fine painting should do no less. Besides providing nurture, place is an important source of our identity—a key to who we are. To the question, "What sort of person are you?" I can imagine the poet W. H. Auden pointing to limestone for answer.[10] Similarly addressed, I would point to the desert. The desert and I are one. In it, I see lineaments of my psychological nature. The arts are likewise emblematic and revelatory. The ones I strongly like and dislike expose me, make me feel naked before the public eye, which is why I am guarded in my confessions.

Of course, place and art also differ. One difference is that, whereas in life I can't go home again, in art I often can. The actual home—a house, neighborhood, town, or city—is likely to be altered by subsequent occupants and their builders. Even the desert will lose its physical integrity as population continues to increase. By contrast, a painting or sculpture, other than the stains and scars of time, stays much the same. To it, I can return. Another difference is that, whereas we are steeped in place, we are always somewhat outside of art. Place is experienced multi-sensorially, art in one or two senses. Knowing a place—and especially knowing the homeplace—is less intellectual than knowing or appreciating (to use that more distancing word) art. Place is more conservative for these reasons. Charles Lamb cannot bear to be anywhere but in his England. Outside England, he is more likely to find deficiencies that diminish his sense of self than novelties that enhance and expand it. Art is a discovery rather than a given: we humans aren't born into art as we are into a home. One discovery in art may well lead to another: Mozart prepares me for Beethoven. The self is static if it is produced by homeplace and only homeplace, flexible and expansive if it is also nurtured by art. Place, too, has the power to open one's eyes to the new. But if so, it is because place—even a familiar place—does not have to be just a soporific cocoon of comforts and habits. Long residence notwithstanding, a home may still have the power to reveal the new in the manner of art. For example, after a violent thunderstorm, one may be surprised by the stillness in the air, enhanced rather than detracted by the music of raindrops falling on a puddle; the vivid, slightly threatening, quality of the yellow sky over the roof; and a renewed appreciation, mixed with gratitude, for a house that stands four-square, undaunted.

PAINTING

In what ways do paintings serve as virtual places, surrogate places? Consider strolling through a picture gallery. The stroll produces fatigue and a sense of futility if there are no paintings worth looking at; in this regard, it is like life, whose winding course can seem listless and barren unless places exist that make us pause in affection, disbelief, or wonder. Of the different genres of painting exhibited in a gallery, is there one that holds special appeal?

Naturally, the answer varies with the individual. I offer mine so that others may be prompted to look into themselves and offer theirs. I tend to pause longer before portraits of people than before pictures of buildings and landscapes. This would be a damning confession for a geographer, except that I see the human being as a special type of place. It is a place to the extent that one can find haven and animal warmth in rounded limbs. Young people prove my point when, in love, they leap over the walls to seek happiness in each other's arms. As for built places, Dutch interiors of the seventeenth century, known to me through Vermeer's paintings, appeal to me for the same reason that they appeal to other members of the propertied middle-class, both in Vermeer's time and in mine. Sunlight pouring into a room full of well-cared for objects—a water jar here, a mandolin there, a map on the wall—invites one to dream of civilized comfort that combines cozy intimacy with hints of a capacious world beyond.

I like deeply humanized landscapes, too. Who doesn't? Constable's contented cows in England's green pastures subtly persuades me that sloth, mildly indulged, may be a virtue. Nevertheless, the landscapes I identify with the most are the strenuous ones of desert and ice.[11] Proof lies in the fact that, whereas only a Vermeer or a Constable will stop me in my track, merely competent renditions of desert and ice can do so, too.

PHOTOGRAPH

Suppose life is a stroll through a gallery of photographs rather than of paintings, what would be the difference? How does the photograph differ from the painting as a virtual place? The subjects depicted may be the same and so the feeling towards them may be similar.

Similar, however, is not same, the difference being a consequence of the viewer's subconscious awareness of how paintings and photographs are made. A photograph is of the moment—an interruption in the flow of time, captured on film, that becomes a stable "place" for one to dwell in and return to should one so wish. Such freezing of a moment was never possible before the invention of the modern camera. Wordsworth, crossing the Alps, very much wanted to retain images of the many scenes that enthralled him, but couldn't.[12] Now we can. When the camera is defective and none of the pictures we have taken on our vacation trip comes out, we feel dismay. Understandably, for without the images and pauses—without these places—it is as though we have not made the trip. Absent experiences that we can hold on to, it could seem that time just sweeps us along, from one moment to the next, and so on to the last one that ushers in death.

Many artists, of course, have attempted to capture the passing moment on canvas. Nevertheless, when we look at the painting of a woman pouring tea, we know we are not catching a moment in the millions that pass in the course of a day, but rather at an image the artist has constructed at leisure in his or her studio. By contrast, when we look at a photograph of the same scene we do so in the belief that, had the camera clicked a second earlier, the woman would have barely lifted the teapot and that, had it clicked a second later, the teapot would have returned to the table.

Three other strains of awareness add to the realism and poignancy of a photograph. One is the sense that the photograph of (say) an old house retains something of the house's physical reality: it was the sunlight of a particular hour and place, and not aesthetic calculation, that worked over the chemically treated film to produce what we see. Second is the awareness that at least some of the details in a photograph—the bird on the telephone wire, the stray paper cup by the telephone stand—are unplanned: they just happen to be there. Third is the awareness of the arbitrariness of a photographic frame:

looking at the photograph of a city street I find myself wondering what the rest of the town looks like, a drift of thought that does not occur when I look at a painting. In other words, I take the painting to be more contained and self-referencing and so, in those regards, more like a bounded geographical place.

POEM

For those who love poetry, a poem invites one to pause, catch up with oneself and the world, before being swept back into the rush of life. As with a painting in the gallery, a poem that is printed and anthologized is always potentially available for one to savor, live in, and return to. Nowhere are these possibilities more eloquently explored than in Wordsworth's "Tintern Abbey." The poem tells of Wordsworth going back to the Wye Valley after an absence of five years to behold once again "these steep and lofty cliffs," "these pastoral farms, green to the very door." So in his time, at least, it was possible to revisit a landscape and find it unchanged. The poem also speaks of a return in imagination. Caught in the dreariness of a town or city, Wordsworth consoles himself with thoughts of a good man's "little, nameless, unremembered acts of kindness and love," and with the memory of a "blessed mood" in which "the heavy and the weary weight of all this unintelligible world is lightened." Wordsworth knows that, even as the Valley remains much the same, he himself has changed and will change. "I cannot paint what I then was." The time is past when the "sounding cataract haunted me like a passion," when "the tall rock, the mountain, and the deep and gloomy wood...were...an appetite." But he does not regret the loss, for other gifts have followed to provide "abundant recompense," one of them being the ability to stand still before "a presence that disturbs [him] with the joy of elevated thoughts; a sense sublime of something far more deeply interfused, whose dwelling is the light of setting suns, and the round ocean, and the living air, and the blue sky, and in the mind of man." Note how place has exploded beyond "pastoral farms green to the very door" to ocean, sky, and the mind of man. Only so can a particular place such as Wye Valley be liberating rather than, in the end, constricting.

NOVEL

What if the art form is not a totality capable of being revealed at once, but is rather something that unfolds sequentially over time? In other words, can a novel that takes hours or even days to read be the same sort of resting place as a poem? A novel that we dutifully plod through is not restful, I submit. It is too much like life—one inconsequential incident after another. Yet, even within such a novel, there may be pages that work on our sensibility as a poem does, making us aware of a presence or mood to which we may wish to return.

I have to confess that I do not willingly re-read a novel from first page to last, no more than I would wish to relive my life in its entirety. But I do return again and again to a particular evocation in a novel, as I do to a particular memory in life. Evocation of what? Sometimes a human encounter, such as that between the two brothers in the Grand Inquisitor chapter of the *Brothers Karamazov;* sometimes a place, such as Peggotty's boathouse at Yarmouth in *David Copperfield*. Even a good novel, however, has few passages that invite the ruminative pause. Most of it—necessarily—is given over to moving characters from here to there, from one event to the next. Indeed, the adventure story demands a fast-moving plot, a clipped narrative pace. My point is, if we ever re-read an adventure story, it cannot be for the plot; it can only be for the atmosphere. By now, I know very well "who done it" in the Sherlock Holmes stories. I know well, too, Holmes's world of London fog and hansom cabs. The plot I may well tire of with repetition, but I do not tire of Holmes's world with greater familiarity, no more than I tire of the familiarity of my home.

MOTION PICTURE

The art of the motion picture compels me to make another confession: although I seldom re-read a novel from beginning to end, I do periodically re-watch an entire film. Why is not immediately clear, for the motion picture, like the novel and life itself, is captive to the relentlessness of sequential time. True, I have a good practical reason to re-watch a film—the need to catch dialogues and gestures that I missed in the first round. Putting it thus suggests that I am interested primarily in the plot. Sometimes this is the case. But not always. Other times I re-watch an entire film in the belief that only then can I recapture the mood of a place—and recapture it more completely than I can if I look only at individual scenes or stills. A movie is rich in incidents; time passes and locations change as they do in a novel and in actual life. What holds the incidents together? What makes a film two to three hours long seem all of a piece? Of course, the incidents and characters may not hold together: films fail in this regard as novels do.

I believe, however, that their success rate is greater because a motion-picture director has two methods of unification at his or her disposal that are unavailable to a novelist. One is color. A director may choose to film in black-and-white, as in François Truffaut's *The Wild Child* (1965), in yellow and brownish hues as in David Lean's *Lawrence of Arabia* (1962), in the whites, blacks, and blues of winter as in Kenneth Branagh's *Hamlet* (1996). A motion picture will not necessarily seem disjointed without a dominant color scheme, but with it a certain character is imparted to the whole that insinuates itself into the viewer's subconscious awareness. The second method available to the film director is sound: he or she can choose a variety of background musics to heighten the emotional charge of a human encounter, place, or landscape, and an overarching theme, played here and there throughout the film, to give the entire story, no matter how diverse its elements, a sense of unity.

François Girard's *The Red Violin* (1998) is an excellent example of the way music can unify the most complex story. Covering a period of three centuries and with dramatic events taking place in locations as varied as Italy, England, China, and Canada, this film of the life history of a musical instrument might be expected to have no coherence at all. Yet it does have coherence, thanks not to the period pieces played on the instrument, but to a central background theme composed by John Corigliano specifically for the film.[13] The music helps to build up a mood that transcends the particularities of place and time. I can imagine someone watching the film again so as to understand the plot better, but I can also imagine someone returning to it for its enthralling mood.

DANCE

Dance is motion, the opposite of stasis—the pause that makes place possible and is its signature. Moreover, dance is heightened or purified motion, which means that it is less well-suited, in comparison with other art forms, to evoking the commonplaces of life. This is an important distinction, for 'home' lies at the center of our conception of a cozy, thickly human place. Consider a woman chopping up cabbage, a man reading the newspaper, and such like activities of daily existence. What arts can incorporate them matter-of-factly, without self-conscious artiness? I would say the pictorial and literary arts. Even of poetry, this is true; and true despite its formal rhymes and vocation for heightened feeling. Dance is the exception.

Home, however, is only one type of place. Other types of place offer surprise and wonder, and have no touch of hominess in them. It is in surprise and wonder that dance comes to its own. The pedestrian flow of time, the gestures and movements of routine life, come to a stop when we look at motion intensified, purified, transfigured that is dance. The word "stop" (like the words "pause" and "stasis") is critical to place. Dance, it goes without saying, is the opposite of stasis. Yet dance, too, becomes "place" when its movements create a temporal pattern that we can apprehend as a whole and of which we feel momentarily a part.

Moreover, within the dance itself, there are breath-catching pauses—"places." Think of the pas-de-deux that culminates in a composite figure of supreme elegance, held for only a second or two; or of a male dancer's leap into space and hanging there in mid-air for, it could seem, longer than is physically possible. These pauses are among the peak moments in classical ballet and modern dance. Paradoxically, they are what motion strives toward, just as one might say, paradoxically, that a goal of music is to give life to its intervals of silence.[14]

MUSIC

Music occurs in time and might be expected to remind listeners of time's inexorable passage. Yet this is not so. Music seems able to annul time, converting it into an atemporal presence, a virtual place, with its insistent beat, as in popular music; its wave-like flow, as in music of the Middle Ages. Strangely enough, this is true even in music imbued with directional energy, as with much that was composed in the early modern period; and music with a story line — say, from "darkness to light"—as was characteristic of Beethoven's heroic style. Despite the arrow-like direction of Beethoven's music, its sense of development, its reaching out to a conclusion of great power, listening to it again and again feels more like re-immersing oneself in a desired presence than following a plot in the hope of learning something new.[15]

Music bears repetition, invites repetition, to a degree unmatched by the pictorial and literary arts. "That's our song," we say nostalgically, but not "that's our landscape painting," or "that's our novel." How many people read a novel, even a favorite one, more than once? How many return to an art gallery a dozen times a year just to see one or two favorite paintings? Yet quite ordinary people, and not just the musically sophisticated, return to the concert hall again and again to listen to a favorite song cycle or symphony. And that explains the wisdom of having a powerful musical theme in a motion picture, for it may well be that what lures the viewer back for a second or third viewing is a mood—a place's atmosphere—that the music helps to create.

Music is home. Like our brick-and-mortar home, we do not tire of returning to it. Yet, unlike that home, whose appeal lies in its familiarity and ordinariness, music is also serenity and exaltation, a soaring of the spirit that is quite out of the ordinary. The mystery of music, then, is that it can be both a place that nurtures the biosocial roots of self, as, for instance, a popular tune laced with spoony lyrics, and pure compositions of sound that, in their unearthly beauty, remind the self that its ultimate dwelling is elsewhere.

If music is home, home is—or can be—music. Thanks to the technologies of recording and production, even a grand parlor can be made to feel tenderly home-like when a child's music box or television is playing a tune from *Sesame Street*; contrariwise, by simply slipping a CD of the Mass in B Minor into a hi-fi set, my cubicle of space is transformed into a cathedral of sound. Where am I then? I am in my living room, confined to an environment of coffee-stained floor and ill-matched chairs, yet also transported to another world—rooted, yet free.

IDENTITY, SELF, AND ULTIMATE PLACE

A faddish slogan since the 1960s is "Back to roots," the idea being that one can't know who one is unless one is rooted in kinfolk and place. I myself find longshoreman Eric Hoffer's view more congenial and true. He notes: "A plant needs roots to grow. With man it is the other way around: only when he grows does he have roots and feel at home in the world."[16]

In pre-modern societies, identity is seldom a worry. People don't go around asking who they are; they know who they are. They are the son or daughter of so-and-so; membership in a lineage and group is the single most important guarantor of identity. Next in importance is occupation: a person is a Smith, Miller, Taylor, Cook, Carpenter, or Wheelwright. Thirdly, one is one's native place—an identification that in Europe seems confined to aristocrats: one is, for example, the Count of Monte Cristo, the Marquess of Milford Haven, or the Duke of Windsor. All these ways of naming, but especially the last two, emphasize social status. A count or a marquess is not someone who possesses marketable skills; he is first and foremost a landowner, and hence he identifies first and foremost with land or place. In a deeper sense, however, everyone does so, if only because ancestral and kinship ties, occupations and the social standings linked to them, all have to exist somewhere and that somewhere is place— and, especially, homeplace.

Back to roots is back to one's homeplace, where group belongingness matters more than an individual's sense of who he or she is. Much of the yearning for roots in the modern and post-modern world is, thus, not so much a yearning for a greater sense of self as a yearning to numb one's troubled self-awareness in group identity. But this is by no means the whole picture. The belief also exists, particularly in the United States, that one's hometown, despite its set ways, can promote individualism. How? Remember that home, to a young child, is not just a familiar place; it is also space, rich in shadowy corners below stairways and in the attic that invite exploration. Beyond home in the narrow sense is the neighborhood, town, and surrounding countryside, a complex arrangement of streets and shops, workplaces and schools, churches and community centers, shaded woods, streams, and water holes. In the United States, nostalgia is directed at this landscape of the recent past. Everyone may feel it in some degree, but American men are likely to feel it most, for, in the early part of the twentieth century, most were able to grow up in a landscape that was safe and yet also full of opportunities for boyish adventure.

Hometown, for all its homely virtues and even because of

them, can stunt growth. Opportunities there for self-discovery may be ample for the growing child, but they do not suffice for the mature human being. Much as American lore praises hometown, it nevertheless has its young men and women abandon it for the larger world. In the larger world, which is usually the city but it could also be the wilderness, they find who they are.[17] Similar lores exist in other societies, a major pre-condition being the fairly common occurrence of upward social mobility. "Who I am is far more than how local place defines me" is the basic idea. For example, had I never left my hometown in humid eastern China, I would never have known my desert personality, never have discovered that the desert—whether in Death Valley or the lands of Acoma Pueblo—is my truer home. And, of course, if I had not savored other countries and cultures, I could never have known my deep affinity for the worlds of Beethoven, C. S. Lewis, Simone Weil, and of motion pictures such as *Gone With the Wind* (1939) and *Les Roseaux Sauvages* (*Wild Reeds*, 1994). These are as much my homes—my sources of comfort and inspiration—as the houses and geographical places I have lived in.

But isn't this multiplicity of homes a sign of personality disintegration? To an outsider it might seem so. Not, however, to me, nor to my friends for whom each confession of a new love on my part causes them initial surprise, only to say, after a pause, "How like you!" The sense I have of myself grows stronger, not weaker, as the number and variety of artworks and places that speak to the core of my being expand. Yet doubts linger, of which two come to the fore. One is the inescapable isolation of the individual—an isolation that increases as a person's individuality is developed and refined. Even as I merge with another in our shared love of Beethoven, I see that *Gone with the Wind* divides us like a Grand Canyon: to me the film is high romance, perhaps because I first saw it as a starry-eyed child, but to one who saw it as an adult, it could seem the sugar-coating of an ignoble past and the worst kind of fantasy.

My second doubt is also widely shared, or should be. It arises from the conviction that life is a serious journey (even a pilgrimage) to a final goal, and not, as it too often is, a Caribbean tour. In such a tour, each port of call may be not only delightful, but also educational in that it enables us to discover both world and self. Yet, in the end, we return to where we started, satiated rather than wiser. Perhaps this is the fuzzy area where geography overlaps with religion; and note that, by religion, I don't mean a particular cultural practice such as the corn dance or *feng shui*; rather I mean the spiritual longing to be elsewhere. Geography is mostly about how we strive to feel at home on Earth, rooted in place; yet, Lamb's and Larkin's claim notwithstanding, we never quite succeed. The arts, too, can be a home, or make us feel more at home. Yet, even more than geographical place, they have the power to disturb or exalt, and so, like the great teachings of religion, remind us that we are fundamentally homeless.

GALLERY OF PHOTOGRAPHS

TAMMY MERCURE

PHOTOGRAPHS OF PLACES IN WISCONSIN AND ILLINOIS

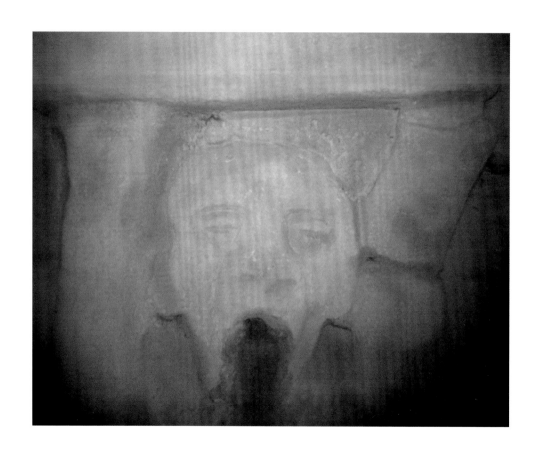

ARTIST'S STATEMENT

One of my favorite places to photograph is the Wisconsin Dells, the most popular tourist mecca in the Midwest. Once upon a time, the Dells was an attraction for the wild river and dramatic bluffs. Then, the natural wonders were supplanted by commercial fantasies. Each resort, restaurant, and tourist amusement tried to compete for attention with appropriated landscapes, miniature world monuments, re-creations of lost civilizations, and bigger-than-life figures from history and mythology. One might stay in a Polynesian hotel and glance out the window to an African jungle miniature golf course. Down the street, one might visit a petting zoo and feed a giraffe or pet a kangaroo. Wisconsin is not an exotic state, and yet in the Wisconsin Dells and in other places near my home in Illinois I have the sense of being on a fantastic excursion. I capture the scenes of this voyage with the historic technique of pinhole photography.

JOCELYN NEVEL

PHOTOGRAPHS OF FOSSILS IN NEW MEXICO

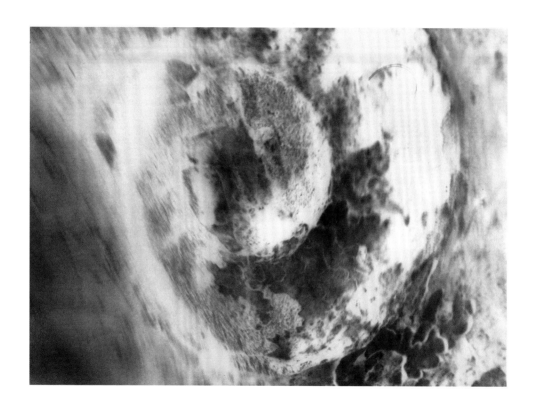

60

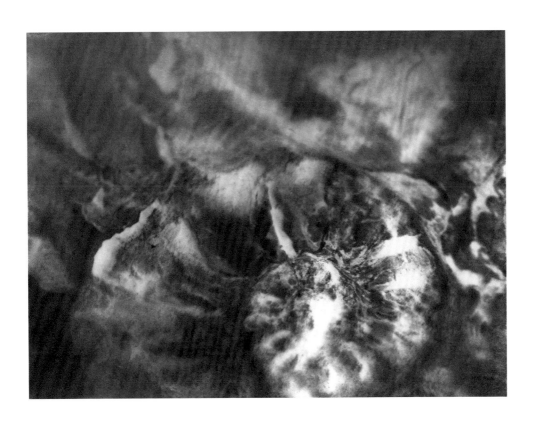

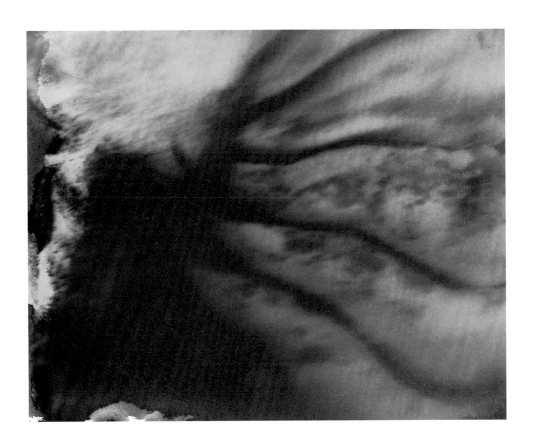

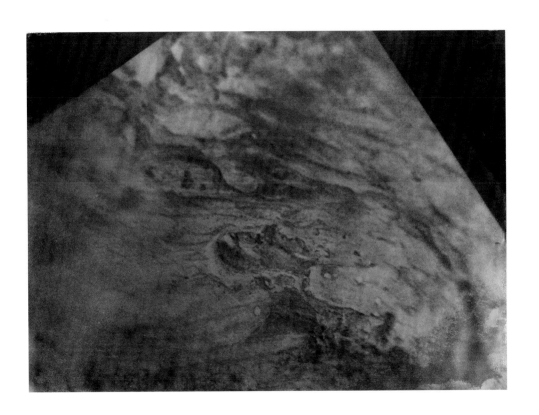

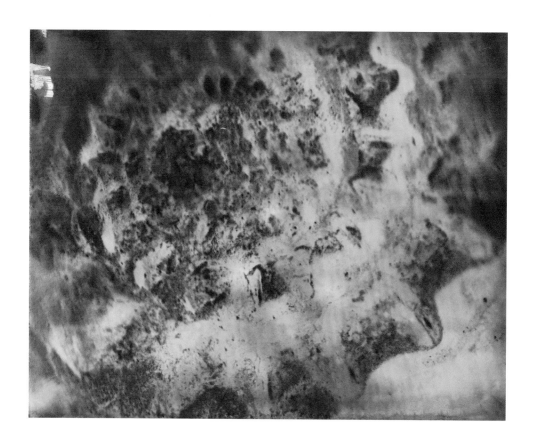

ARTIST'S STATEMENT

When I arrived in New Mexico in August of 2000, I quickly became fascinated by the near absence of water. I began to think about different geological periods when the Southwest was not only covered by an ocean and vast lakes, but also populated by very different life. I began to photograph specimens from the fossil collection of the Department of Earth and Planetary Sciences at the University of New Mexico. Initially I was most fascinated and engaged with the repetition of the spiral, particularly found in *ammonoids*, a bivalve found in the Cretaceous era. To create a more complete study I also documented specimens such as *crinoids* and fields of texture found in strata, which might contain multiple fossils. A comprehensive search of the fossil record allowed me to express a more complex depiction of oceanic life in a present-day desert environment.

In all my work I am interested in bringing various matter or detritus back to life. These fossils are re-presented through an artistic process, which includes coating a wet emulsion on paper, then exposing that paper to bright sunlight, and drying it while blowing in the wind on my clothesline. The earth, stone, air, and water all transpired to create these fossil subjects. I have again used these elements to create this series: *Aquosus (Abounding in Water)*.

JOHN WILLIS AND TOM YOUNG

PHOTOGRAPHS OF A PAPER RECYCLING PLANT IN MASSACHUSETTS

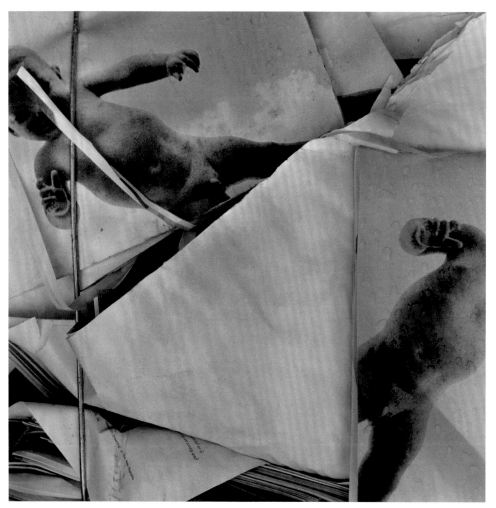

ARTISTS' STATEMENT

Alongside a winding river in the seemingly pristine hills of western Massachusetts sits a paper recycling plant where these photographs were made. In ways both disturbing and intriguing, the rural landscape of forested hills has been transformed into a landscape of bales of discarded paper. This paper carries images and text from popular culture, and is formed into a new topography with lingering evidence of its past existence.

We are interested in this transformation from a living forest to a constructed representation of human activity. While photographing at this site we are aware of the temporary nature of this landscape. It is a repository about to be reconditioned into yet another consumer product. The images of people and culture buried in the stacks of paper call out to us, and beg us to look within, at our transitory existence, and also to consider the fragile natural world that surrounds this site. This connection of self with the world is one of the most comfortable, most familiar, and most grounding experiences we can have.

NOTES

1. David Cecil, *Literary Looking Glass: A Personal Anthology* (London: Constable, 1975), p. 48.

2. Philip Larkin, *Required Writing* (Ann Arbor: University of Michigan Press, 1999), p. 55.

3. Hugo Williams, *All the Time in the World* (Pleasantville, NY: Alkadian Press, 1997), pp. 12, 33-34.

4. Fridtjof Nansen, *Farthest North: Being the Record of a Voyage of Exploration of the Ship "Fram," 1893-96* (New York: Harper & Brothers, 1897), vol. 1, p. 81.

5. Nansen, *Farthest North,* vol. 2, p. 446.

6. Christopher Ralling, *Shackleton: His Antarctic Writings* (London: British Broadcasting Corporation, 1983), p. 79.

7. As told in the *New York Times,* 1 September 200l.

8. The meaning of *place* is primarily positive, and I have chosen to emphasize that in this essay, but, of course, its meaning can also be strongly negative: one needs only to think of a prison, concentration camp, dysfunctional home, or dismal swamp. Art is positive in the sense that it is the creation of order out of chaos, though Morse Peckham would probably prefer to say that it is exposing people to a manageable and, therefore, liberating chaos. Either way, art remains positive. See Morse Peckham, *Man's Rage for Chaos* (New York: Schocken Books, 1967).

9. Hanna Kiel, ed., *The Bernard Berenson Treasury* (New York: Simon & Schuster, 1962), p. 92.

10. Landscape of Eden is "Limestone uplands like the Pennines...," W. H. Auden, *The Dyer's Hand and Other Essays* (New York: Random House, 1962), p. 6. See, also, the poem, "In Praise of Limestone" (1948).

11. Yi-Fu Tuan, "Desert and Ice: Ambivalent Aesthetics," in Salim Kemal and Ivan Gaskell, eds., *Landscape, Natural Beauty, and the Arts* (Cambridge: Cambridge University Press, 1993), pp. 139-157; "The Desert and I: A Study in Affinity," *Michigan Quarterly Review*, Winter 2001, pp. 7-16.

12. Stephen Gill, *Wordsworth: A Life* (New York: Oxford University Press, 1989), p. 48.

13. "Provenance: John Corigliano on The Red Violin," in David Morgan, ed., *Knowing the Score* (New York: HarperCollins, 2000), pp. 258-266.

14. In the film, *Billy Elliot* (2000), the last scene shows Billy, as the White Swan, leaping into space to the soaring music of Tchaikovsky. He freezes in mid-air, and that's the end of the film—appropriately, for we spectators see it as the perfect moment and his place in the air the perfect place, and do not wish him to come down to Earth, however gracefully, to complete the dance pattern, much less to return to the dressing room, put on a sweater and a pair of pants, and continue with ordinary life.

15. Agnes Crawford Schuldt, "The Voices of Time in Music," *The American Scholar*, Autumn 1976, pp. 549-559; Scott Burnham, *Beethoven Hero* (Princeton: Princeton University Press, 1995), pp. 163-165; Lewis Lockwood, *Beethoven: The Music and the Life* (New York: Norton, 2003), p. 224.

16. Eric Hoffer, *Reflections on the Human Condition* (New York: Harper & Row, 1972), p. 80.

17. Page Smith, *As a City upon a Hill: The Town in American History* (Cambridge: MIT Press, 1973).

ABOUT THE ARTISTS

TAMMY MERCURE has exhibited throughout the Midwest, including solo shows at the Chicago Cultural Center in Illinois and the Sioux City Art Center in Iowa. She has received numerous awards and grants, including a Polaroid Artist Support Grant and several CAAP Grants from the City of Chicago. Her work is included in several collections and is represented in the Midwest Photographers Project at the Museum of Contemporary Photography. She currently resides in Chicago and is the Digital Imaging Facilities Coordinator for the Columbia College Chicago Photography Department where she received her B.A. **www.tammymercure.com**

JOCELYN NEVEL received her M.F.A. in photography from Columbia College Chicago. In 1999 she received a commission from Disney Enterprises to make a large-scale sculptural quilt about the White Sox for the ESPN Zone. Ms. Nevel has also received three City Arts Assistance Grants from the City of Chicago. In 1998 and 1999 she taught at The School of the Art Institute of Chicago and was an artist-in-residence in the Photography Department of Columbia College Chicago. In 2000 she was a visiting assistant professor in the Art Department at Cornell University, and since 2001 she has been an assistant professor in the Art and Art History Department at the University of New Mexico. Ms. Nevel exhibits nationally in solo and group exhibitions. **www.jocelynnevel.com**

JOHN WILLIS received his M.F.A. in photography from the Rhode Island School of Design in 1986. He has received grants from the Vermont Arts Endowment and four grants from the Vermont Arts Council. His work is included in many public and private collections, including the Whitney Museum of American Art and the Houston Museum of Fine Arts. He has exhibited frequently nationally and internationally during the past twenty years. Mr. Willis's work has also been widely published in photographic books and journals. Mr. Willis is currently a professor of art at Marlboro College and co-founder of the In-Sight Photography Project.
jwillis@marlboro.edu

TOM YOUNG received his M.F.A. in photography from the Rhode Island School of Design in 1977. He has been awarded an Artist Fellowship from the National Endowment for the Arts and four Artist Fellowships from the Massachusetts Cultural Council. His work is included in numerous permanent print collections, including the Museum of Fine Arts in Boston, the Polaroid International Collection, and Harvard University's Fogg Museum. Best known for his landscape photographs that address personal narrative, Young has had more than seventy exhibits internationally, and his photographs have appeared in numerous publications. Mr. Young is currently a professor of art at Greenfield Community College in Greenfield, Massachusetts. **youngart@rcn.com**